A TIME TO FLY

HOW TO FEEL GOOD ABOUT OURSELVES AND OUR RELATIONSHIPS

Ellie Janow, M.S., C.E.D.T.
Illustrated by Robert P. Zangrillo

CELESTIAL ARTS
BERKELEY, CALIFORNIA

Copyright © 1987, 1993 by Ellie Janow. All rights reserved. No part of this book may be reproduced in any form, except for brief review, without the written permission of the publisher. For information write: Celestial Arts Publishing, Post Office Box 7123, Berkeley, California 94707. Printed in the United States of America.

Text design and typography by Mary McDermott
Cover design by Fifth Street Design
Illustrations by Robert P. Zangrillo

"A Time to Fly" by Diane Schorr is used with the gracious permission of the author.

FIRST CELESTIAL ARTS PRINTING 1993

Library of Congress Cataloging-in-Publication Data

Janow, Ellie.
    A time to fly : how to feel good about ourselves and our relationships / Ellie Janow ; illustrated by Robert P. Zangrillo.
       p.   cm.
    ISBN 0-89087-684-3 $7.95
    1. Self-actualization (Psychology) 2. Interpersonal relations. 3. Self-acceptance. 4. Course in miracles. I. Title.
BF637.S4J36 1993   92-32741
158 - - dc20   CIP

1 2   3   4   5   6   7   8   9   10 /   97 96 95 94 93

DEDICATION

*This book is dedicated
to my husband, Herb, who
has been my loving teacher.*

*His unconditional acceptance
has inspired me to be
all that I can be.*

*With special thanks to my children,
my family, and my friends. I am deeply
grateful for their many hours of
listening, sharing, and caring.*

CONTENTS

AUTHOR'S STORY AND INTRODUCTION *ix*

CHAPTER I   WHAT'S KEEPING US FROM FLYING *3*

    The Blocks of Anger, Guilt, and Fear 6
    Am I a Victim? 11
    Personal Inventory 13
    It's Been My Choice 33

CHAPTER II   I CAN FLY IF I SEE THINGS DIFFERENTLY *39*

    Changing Our Thinking Is the Key to Our Freedom 43
    Getting Rid of a Negative Belief 48
    Taking Responsibility 51
    What Have I Learned So Far? 53
    Seeing Only Love 54
    Forgiveness 60

CHAPTER III   BLAST OFF TO FREEDOM WITH MIRACLES *67*

    Choosing Love Will Dissipate the Block of Anger 69
    Choosing Love Will Eliminate the Block of Fear 73
    Choosing Love Will Alleviate the Block of Guilt 77

CHAPTER IV   KEEP FLYING HIGH *87*

    Affirming Our Peace and Freedom 88
    Visualizing Our Serenity and Joy 92
    Sharing Our Growth and Love 97
    Daily Positive Checklist 104

EPILOGUE   THE CHANGELING EAGLE *107*

A time to fly
  To grow to soar
  To live to love
    And be myself

A time to fly
  To reach the stars
  To feel the warmth
    From deep within

A time to fly
  To be at peace
  To reawaken
    With each new dawn

DIANE SCHORR

AUTHOR'S STORY AND INTRODUCTION

Although I was living the American dream, I knew I was falling into a black hole. I had become the victim of a vicious cycle of fear, anger, and guilt that started as far back as I can remember.

I strived to be a "perfect" daughter, "perfect" student, and "perfect" friend, wanting to be good so everyone would love me. I always tried to do the "right" thing, then looked around for that pat on the head from mom or teacher, waiting for them to say, "Ellie, you're OK." I learned early to size up people, sense what they expected from me, and give it to them in order to attain my reward of acceptance. The worst fears were that I would be rejected because I wasn't good enough and that my behavior would be judged as disappointing.

I always masked my face with a smile to keep anyone from knowing my true feelings and to cover up the resentments that built up as I "people pleased." I wanted to control situations, needing to appear confident. I filled my life with things, achieving all in a frenzy, then rated myself after accomplishing multiple difficult tasks. My favorite pastime was complaining to my friends about how I had handled all my pressures in spite of endless responsibilities; I loved the strokes of, "Oh, Ellie, I don't know how you do it. You're so special." If only they knew and I knew how, needing validation of my self-worth, I unconsciously set up these almost impossible tasks to prove to myself and to them how terrific I was.

I did what was expected of me, without questioning. I married, had children, and spent every waking moment making sure that we presented to the world the picture of the "perfect" American family. I was so busy attaining my goals of having my "perfectly" furnished, immaculate home, juggling working and homemaking, helping with the homework, being the "perfect" wife, lover, and playmate, there was no time to be loving or to enjoy time spent with my family.

Eventually I asked myself, "Why am I always yelling? Why do I eat compulsively? Why do I have a tantrum if one unexpected, unexplained thing happens to upset my routine? Why do I always have to be right and to manipulate to get my way? Why do I feel so exhausted, feel like such a phony, feel so unworthy and at the same time feel hyper, judgmental, and superior, almost Godlike? Who am I and am I ever going to fill this emptiness in my gut?"

That black hole was engulfing me and I believed I had no choice. If I had five happy experiences and one painful experience, I would zero in and feel bad about the negative, completely disregarding any of the positives. The guilt about everything immobilized me. I thought that my family didn't love me, and that they listened to me only because they were afraid of my "mouth." I had learned to feel ugly and fat and I yearned to feel beautiful. Inside, I was scared about what was going to happen; on the outside, I wore the mask of a person in control, who was to be respected. My inside did not match my outside. I felt isolated and misunderstood. I was at my emotional bottom.

I had spent my life waiting for a person, place, or thing to make me happy. I had achieved it all, and I still wasn't happy. I was successful professionally, a speech/language pathologist in private practice, and was a mother of two healthy daughters, with a loving, considerate husband. I was affluent materially and in good health. Still, I was experiencing constant disappointment, frustration, self-pity, and resentment. I was unable to enjoy or cope effectively with my life.

Thinking that "being thin" would be the missing ingredient to my well-being, I joined a self-help program for my overeating. With thinness as my only goal, I followed the diet part of the program "perfectly" and lost weight. To my dismay, my life did not change: I was still miserable. However, instead of gaining my weight back, I kept going to meetings with an open mind, and I was guided through a process of recovery from negative thinking and chaos.

I learned that I was eating over what was eating me. I discovered that my body reflected my inner attitudes and feelings, and that my excessive eating was a symptom of the need to correct those attitudes. In order to recover, I had to be willing to give up my old ideas. By embracing a more loving attitude, taught in the program, I started to feel good about myself, and I was willing, as a way of life, to abstain from the foods that were not healthy for me. Miraculously, I have maintained my normal body weight and my sanity, one day at a time, for the past fourteen years.

My quest for truth also led me to *A Course in Miracles,* a text, workbook, and manual for teachers, which enhanced the spiritual principles I was already learning in the self-help program. Its philosophy and daily mental and experiential exercises aim at changing our perception of the world, which changes how we feel. It is a process of releasing fear, anger, and guilt by using the power of love that lies within each of us to become peaceful and free.

There is a story of a ballet dancer who, when he went to his first ballet class, told the teacher, "I want to fly." The teacher replied, "Now, let's go to the exercise bar. You have to free yourself so you can fly."

We can fly, but like that dancer, we must let go of whatever is preventing us from being free. We have to release our minds of all our fear, guilt, and anger because that's what is stopping us from being ourselves, the loving, peaceful, forgiving people we truly are.

I've tried the conventional ways to dissipate my anger and guilt. I counted to ten, reasoned, banged on a pillow, and through therapy discovered why I was angry, resentful, fearful, and guilty. I even told people how I felt, in a calm manner, but my rage still seethed within and my guilt persisted. None of these remedies worked for me. I needed a more drastic, yet simple, means of finding joy and inner peace.

After endless searching, I have found a solution based on forgiveness and love, and it works. I have been healing myself and my relationships by tapping the power of love within me. Sometimes I forget to call upon this inner guidance and I feel pain, but I learn lessons and I grow. I treat my lapses of memory with gentleness and a sense of humor, then continue on my spiritual path with that emptiness gone from my gut. And that's progress.

Let me share my awareness and growth with you. The details of your life may be differcnt from mine, but we may share the same feelings, and we can share the same recovery.

The following pages reflect a step-by-step process from fear to freedom. This book is the result of many years of learning, growing, loving, sharing, and flying. I love the journey, and this is for you.

WHAT'S KEEPING US FROM FLYING

*If we always do
what we've always done,
we'll always get
what we've always gotten.*

CHAPTER 1

Most of us are totally oblivious to our feelings. We react to outside stimuli, unaware that we have choices. We are unaware that within our minds there are two voices that talk to us. There is a willful child voice that says, *Don't trust anyone. Defend yourself at all times, they're out to get you. Feel guilty, you are unworthy. Be chaotic, be confused. Get angry, they are the enemy!*

There is also a loving voice that says, *Be joyful, be peaceful. It's OK. You can do it! Stay in the moment. Enjoy people. We are uniquely the same. Be who you are!*

We think that we are victims, that we have no choices because the only voice we have heard is the willful child's. If we are not happy, and if we want different results, we have to change our thinking and learn to trust the loving voice that has been inside us all the time.

We can train our minds to hear that inner peaceful voice and choose to listen to its guidance. When we decide to choose love instead of chaos, we become free and we can fly. But first, we must discover what is keeping us from flying. What exactly are these blocks that cover up our real loving selves?

WITHIN OUR MINDS THERE ARE TWO VOICES THAT TALK TO US

THE BLOCKS OF ANGER, GUILT, AND FEAR

ANGER   When we believe someone or something attacks, deprives, or disappoints us in any area, we experience and express anger in the forms of rage, hostility, striking out with verbal abuse or physical violence, temper tantrums, sarcasm, teasing, and even deadly silence because we want people and things to be different. The anger gives us a feeling of superiority and control because we believe we have the right to be angry. Anger is not our natural state. It is a learned reaction to frustration which we judge as unhealthy for us, but we continue to abuse ourselves with it.

GUILT   Guilt is the same as anger, but the opposite side of the coin. When we believe that we have hurt, deprived, disappointed, or attacked an individual, society, or ourselves, we focus on the event, feel angry, and judge ourselves for what we did or should have done, said, or thought. This occurs especially when we haven't adhered to behaviors and attitudes taught to us in childhood. Guilt keeps us immobilized. It is self-inflicted and serves the purpose of validating our lack of self-worth by reminding us that we don't deserve to be happy, to be successful, or to be loved.

Unfortunately, all the guilt in the world cannot change past behavior, so the physical stress and mental torture serve no purpose. There is a misconception that our guilt will prevent us from making the same mistake again or "we will cheat with guilt," so our behavior won't get out of hand.

We think the guilt will keep it in check. Guilt, however, actually increases our chances of repeating negative behavior. For example: We do something and feel guilty. The feeling of guilt is our punishment. Therefore we are absolved, so we have permission to do it again.

Please note that simply learning from a mistake, feeling uncomfortable and vowing to avoid its repetition, is not guilt, but is a necessary part of growth.

FEAR Fear is a feeling of anxiety and agitation caused by the presence or anticipation of danger, usually imagined. We experience fear of the unknown, which manifests itself in rigidity and resistance to change. We experience fear of failure, which leads to a quest for perfection in ourselves and in others, or to wearing masks, or to "people pleasing," or to not even trying. Other fears are:

>fear of loss of financial security
>
>fear of loss of prestige or self-esteem
>
>fear of not being loved
>
>fear of losing the person we wish to possess (jealousy)
>
>fear of being thin/fat
>
>fear of death or illness for oneself and loved ones
>
>fear of intimacy/sex/sexuality
>
>fear of authority
>
>fear of being separate
>
>fear of rejection/abandonment

GET RID OF THE BLOCKS AND LET THE LOVING SPIRIT WITHIN YOU SHINE THROUGH

Fear, guilt, and anger are so interrelated that they form a vicious cycle. As illustrated on page 10 our reaction to fear triggers our guilt, which we express as anger. These emotions signal the absence of love, and they are all lies. They are an elaborate system of defenses that make us feel bad. We don't need them. Their only function is to block the loving people we truly are.

On the flip side, however, there is a wondrous circle of freedom in which love, forgiveness, and serenity are so interrelated that they trigger each other in a similar fashion.

We have been so busy playing the victim, traveling in the vicious cycle of fear, anger, and guilt, building up blocks of negative feelings, that not only are we unable to hear our loving voice, we don't believe joy and peace are possible for us. They are possible at this very moment, if we want them.

This is how the vicious cycle works: Sally has a fear of failure that she learned as a child, so she strives for perfection in all that she does. After receiving a B+ in a course at a nearby community college, Sally came home and yelled at her husband for not getting a promotion and at her son for failing to make varsity. You see, when Sally makes a mistake, her willful child voice will shout, *You are unworthy,* and Sally feels guilty about it. This judgment of herself makes her angry, and because it's difficult to accept responsibility for that anger, it's easier to criticize her husband and her son for their mistakes. By doing this, she can express her anger justifiably, thinking *He made me angry because he is a failure.* It is really her insecurities being projected onto others. Then she feels guilty because she has attacked them, and the vicious cycle goes on and on. All Sally really wants is to be loving, but she doesn't hear her inner loving voice that says, *It's OK to make mistakes.* That voice is being blocked by the fear she projects onto everything she experiences.

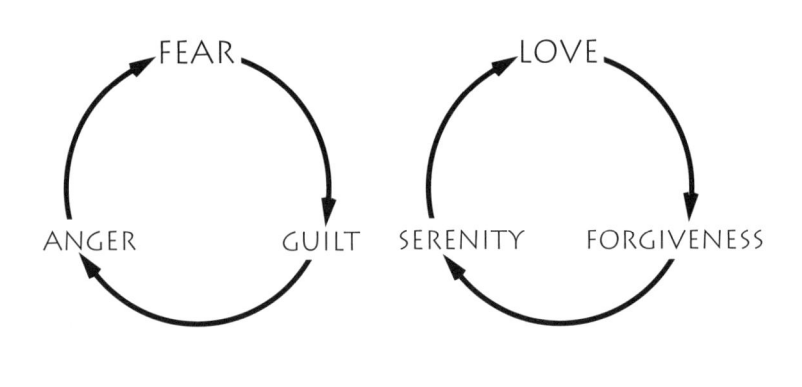

```
        FEAR                    LOVE

  ANGER      GUILT      SERENITY    FORGIVENESS
```

THE VICIOUS CYCLE   **THE CIRCLE OF FREEDOM**

AM I A VICTIM?

I traveled in the vicious cycle. At times, I still do. Whether you are aware of it or not, so do you. Before we can become free, we have to identify exactly what our specific blocks are.

Phase One of our journey to freedom is to make ourselves aware of how we operate by taking a written inventory of our feelings.

When I approached this Personal Inventory, I was afraid of the pain; afraid to bring up old wounds; afraid that I would be overwhelmed by how bad I was. I was worried that I would get depressed when I saw honestly how I was behaving. What if I didn't have the courage to change? Would I see myself as weak?

It was pointed out to me that I was using fear to block my self-discovery and growth. I was reassured that my psyche would not allow me to reveal anything I couldn't handle. It would keep suppressed and buried whatever was too painful. They were right.

As an added guarantee, I wrote the following statement on top of each page of my inventory:

> *I'm admitting to these shortcomings*
> *in hopes of getting to know myself*
> *without judgment.*
>
> *I release all negativity*
> *attached to each situation.*
> *I love and accept myself just the way I am.*
>
> **Write it even if you don't mean it.**

If I started to condemn myself for past behavior, I switched to the positive portion of the inventory as a balance. If you fill in the following Personal Inventory, you will have a chance to acknowledge the guilt, anger, and fear as well as the good feelings permeating your life. Be honest; don't be hard on yourself if you are not happy with your discoveries. Remember, your feelings aren't unique. We are all the same—the commas are just in different places. Find a quiet spot with no distractions. Do a little at a time, whatever is comfortable for you.

Begin with the block that gives you the most difficulty or with the inventory of positive feelings. The following pages are only outlines to stimulate your thinking. Don't limit yourself. Write your feelings down in any form, in any way. Make your list as sketchy or as thorough as you like. Just do it and keep it handy for further reference. I discovered I was only as sick as my secrets. We need to take stock of our feelings to know where we are so we can get where we want to be. The truth will set us free. Good luck!

PERSONAL INVENTORY OF ANGER

STATEMENT: *I felt angry when...*

My mother   DISAPPOINTED *me by reneging on money promised for house*
_____
_____
_____

JUDGED
_____
_____
_____

CRITICIZED
_____
_____
_____

PHYSICALLY ATTACKED
_____
_____
_____

VERBALLY ABUSED
_____
_____
_____

RESENTED
_____
_____
_____

SEXUALLY ABUSED
_____
_____
_____

PERSONAL INVENTORY OF ANGER

STATEMENT: *I felt angry when...*

DEPRIVED

_____
_____
_____

NEGLECTED

_____
_____
_____

CHEATED

_____
_____
_____

STOLE

_____
_____
_____

REJECTED

_____
_____
_____

FORCED

_____
_____
_____

EMBARRASSED

_____
_____
_____

FAILED

MANIPULATED

CONTROLLED

EXPOSED

TEASED

ABANDONED

COMPULSIVELY USED

DEPENDED ON

LOVING SPIRIT HUGH SAYS

DON'T JUST READ IT
LIVE IT!

PERSONAL INVENTORY OF GUILT

STATEMENT: *I felt guilty when I...*

DISAPPOINTED — *my son by working full-time so I couldn't be there for him after school with milk and cookies*

JUDGED

CRITICIZED

PHYSICALLY ATTACKED

VERBALLY ABUSED

REJECTED

FORCED

PERSONAL INVENTORY OF GUILT

STATEMENT: *I felt guilty when I…*

EMBARRASSED
_____
_____
_____

FAILED
_____
_____
_____

MANIPULATED
_____
_____
_____

CONTROLLED
_____
_____
_____

SEXUALLY ABUSED
_____
_____
_____

DEPRIVED
_____
_____
_____

NEGLECTED
_____
_____
_____

CHEATED

STOLE

RESENTED

EXPOSED

TEASED

ABANDONED

COMPULSIVELY USED

DEPENDED ON

LOVING SPIRIT HUGH SAYS

DON'T JUST READ IT
LIVE IT!

PERSONAL INVENTORY OF FEAR

STATEMENT: *I have a fear of being...*

DISAPPOINTED   *so I don't trust anyone*
_____
_____
_____

JUDGED
_____
_____
_____

CRITICIZED
_____
_____
_____

PHYSICALLY ATTACKED
_____
_____
_____

VERBALLY ABUSED
_____
_____
_____

SEXUALLY ABUSED
_____
_____
_____

DEPRIVED
_____
_____
_____

PERSONAL INVENTORY OF FEAR

STATEMENT: *I have a fear of being...*

NEGLECTED
_____
_____
_____

CHEATED
_____
_____
_____

STOLEN FROM
_____
_____
_____

RESENTED
_____
_____
_____

REJECTED
_____
_____
_____

FORCED TO
_____
_____
_____

EMBARRASSED
_____
_____
_____

A FAILURE
_____
_____
_____

MANIPULATED
_____
_____
_____

CONTROLLED
_____
_____
_____

EXPOSED
_____
_____
_____

COMPULSIVE WITH
_____
_____
_____

TEASED
_____
_____
_____

DEPENDED ON
_____
_____
_____

ABANDONED
_____
_____
_____

LOVING SPIRIT HUGH SAYS

DON'T JUST READ IT
LIVE IT!

PERSONAL INVENTORY OF LOVE, FORGIVENESS AND SERENITY

STATEMENT: *I felt good about...*

MY KINDNESS *toward my neighbor when she was hospitalized. I watched her children. I didn't disappoint her.*

MY FORGIVENESS OF

MY SERENITY WHEN

MY LOVING ATTITUDE TOWARD

MY ACCEPTANCE OF

MY POSITIVE OUTLOOK ABOUT

MY OPEN-MINDEDNESS IN REGARD TO

MY WILLINGNESS TO IMPROVE MYSELF WHEN
_____
_____
_____

MY PHYSICAL ATTRIBUTES OF
_____
_____
_____

MY ATHLETIC ABILITIES IN
_____
_____
_____

MY RELATIONSHIPS WITH
_____
_____
_____

MY SENSE OF HUMOR WHEN
_____
_____
_____

MY IMAGINATION WHEN
_____
_____
_____

MY HONESTY ABOUT
_____
_____
_____

MY GENEROSITY WITH
_____
_____
_____

MY PATIENCE WITH _____
_____
_____

BEING HELPFUL TOWARD _____
_____
_____

BEING TALENTED IN _____
_____
_____

MY LEISURE-TIME ACTIVITY WHEN _____
_____
_____

MY JOB/PROFESSION BECAUSE _____
_____
_____

MY TOLERANCE OF _____
_____
_____

MY WILLINGNESS TO TAKE A RISK WHEN _____
_____
_____

MY KNOWLEDGE ABOUT _____
_____

Now that wasn't so bad...

If you're anything like me, you've probably discovered that listing the negatives is much easier than recording our attributes. Most of us find very little to feel good about because we have been programmed to feel bad. We tend to concentrate on our shortcomings and to disregard the positive qualities we all share. Don't worry! The seven phases presented in this book will help you feel better about yourself and your relationships. As you progress through the phases you will make more daily positive checklists; you will be amazed at how many new, wonderful feelings and deeds you will then be able to appreciate about yourself.

When you review the negative-feelings section of the inventory you just completed, notice that you get angry and feel guilty in the areas where you have the most fear. If you fear rejection, you have probably listed numerous people with whom you are angry because they rejected you and you have admitted to guilty feelings over your rejection of others. This is common to us all. However, instead of acknowledging these feelings and letting them go, we harbor them until they fester and block the wonderful, loving feelings hidden beneath our self-imprisoning shields.

Is it any wonder that we are in pain, that we are immobilized and feel like victims? Our fear triggers our guilt and anger, trapping us in the vicious cycle.

Do you want to change—to travel in the circle of freedom, or would you like to continue being a victim, as illustrated by Bob, Bella, Jeff, and Sid in the following stories?

BOB'S STORY

I feel guilty that I'm being unfaithful to my wife. Because I'm lying to her, I'm going against my moral upbringing, and I'm afraid that she will leave me if she finds out about it. I don't want to lose her trust, and besides, I don't want to be alone. It makes me angry that she is not more attractive. I wish she were more loving and understanding. I deserve more appreciation than that. Can't you see that it's her fault I'm looking outside of my marriage? I'm sorry, but I can't stop. I need the warmth and excitement of my other relationship. So why do I feel so guilty? I can't leave her or my children. Poor me! I'm a victim.

BELLA'S STORY

So I'm a little overweight. There are times when I'm afraid I'll get fatter. I know it's unhealthy, and I know that my husband no longer finds me attractive. That really scares me. I hate the way I look and suspect my children are ashamed of me. Out of desperation, I recently went on a diet. I was furious because I couldn't eat the food I wanted when I wanted it. To top it off, it seems that the whole world is sabotaging me with delicious temptations, which is really unfair. So I had a little ice cream to make me feel better, which made me spoil a perfect week on my diet. I felt guilty about it so I ate some more, which made me angrier. Then I got disgusted with myself and binged on a bag of Oreo cookies, which made me more guilty and more fearful that I'm never going to lose weight. You know, sometimes I feel I'm afraid to get thin. Poor me! I'm a victim of my obesity.

JEFF'S STORY

I'm sixteen years old. I hate living at home because my parents are constantly criticizing me and calling me lazy. Boy, I must really be a failure because I try really hard in school, yet nothing I do is good enough for them. That really makes me mad. They hate my friends, and Dad says that I don't appreciate what he does for me. It doesn't even pay for me to study any more because Mom says that I'll never amount to anything anyway. I'm such a disappointment to them. They probably don't love me anymore, and I'm afraid they'll reject me. The only thing I can do is to protect myself and get angry at them before they get down on me. This makes them angrier and makes me guiltier and more afraid. Poor me! I'm a victim.

SID'S STORY

I was offered a new job. I'm frightened that I'm not qualified to do the administrative work required. I really don't want the job anyway because it's mostly paperwork and I know I can be a great salesman. My wife keeps nagging me to take it because the salary is excellent and she wants to quit work to have a baby. I'm afraid to make any decision because if I don't take the job, my wife will make me feel guilty. If I do take the job, I won't be happy because I don't really want it. Poor me! I'm a victim.

In the preceding stories, the characters felt they were victims. Victims believe they aren't responsible for their unhappiness. They are trapped and can't change their situations because they are just innocent, helpless bystanders. People, places, and things are making them feel fearful, angry, and guilty. They find others who will sympathize with their tales of woe so they can stay in the problem, feel justified in their resentments toward people and themselves, and not look for solutions.

As long as Bob, Bella, Jeff, and Sid believe they are victims, they will remain in the vicious cycle of fear, anger, and guilt. Their only escape lies in the realization that they have chosen to feel that way.

When Bob stops blaming his wife for his affair, he may be able to discover his part in the breakdown of communication in his marriage. He may be able to make his marriage better, end it, or choose to continue the affair with less fear, anger, and guilt, taking full responsibility for his actions and knowing he did his best.

When Bella realizes that she is not a victim but is choosing to eat instead of coping with her life, she may find many options open to her.

She may discover that although she is not ready to deal with her problems right away she can choose to accept her overweight body until the time is right to lose weight; this decision in itself will lessen her fear, anger, and guilt.

She may decide to change her way of eating to low fat foods and smaller portions, but this time, when she deviates from her healthy plan, she can take responsibility, forgive herself for not being perfect, and continue her healthy way of eating instead of using her imperfections as an excuse to binge.

She may decide to combine going to a certified therapist/counselor for professional help, with nutritional counseling and/or attend a self-help support group. These choices will help her deal with her fear, anger, and guilt as well as her addiction to food. As she learns to lead a fulfilling life with love, she will no longer need to eat over her feelings.

When Jeff stops thinking of himself as a victim and notices that his reactions to his parents' criticism and judgment have kept him in the cycle of fear, anger, and guilt, many new options will be open to him.

He may discover that he no longer chooses to work so hard for his parents' approval since he may never achieve recognition in their eyes and strive instead to appreciate himself. He may decide to see his parents differently, as unhappy people doing the best they know how, who are taking out their own frustrations on him. With this change of perception, Jeff no longer has to accept his parents' judgments of him as truth.

He may risk sharing his problems of rejection with his parents and make them aware of his pain. This could result in professional family counseling, or better communication, or no change except for Jeff's relief that he has expressed his feelings honestly, lessening his fear, anger, and guilt.

When Sid stops blaming his wife for his unhappiness he may discover his own part in his inability to make a career decision. When he owns his fear, anger, and guilt, he may decide against taking the new administrative position or may risk trying it, hoping to learn on the job; perhaps he will change careers altogether and be the salesman he has dreamed of being. All of these options are open to him when he is no longer a victim because he has a choice to say no or to say yes, make mistakes, learn from them, and try again.

IT'S BEEN MY CHOICE

The details of your life may be different from Bob's, Bella's, Jeff's, and Sid's, but the feelings are the same. So now what? Have you enjoyed guilt and fear? Do you feel justified seething in self-righteous anger? Would you rather be right or peaceful?

When we hold on to grudges, we are the ones in pain. You can stop your despair right now and start breaking out of the vicious cycle by saying to yourself, as I did, "I'm choosing the anger; I'm choosing the guilt; I'm responsible for my feelings." We are whole and complete right now. We don't have to blame others for our distress or to wait for them to change so we can be at peace. The answers are not out there, but within us.

Experience Phase Two of our journey to freedom by practicing owning your feelings. Refer to the inventory you just filled out. Look at each experience and say methodically, "In each instance I had a choice. I didn't have to respond with fear, guilt, or anger." Be prepared to look at each event from an entirely different angle. Relist each person's positive and negative qualities. Try not to dwell on the individual's defects of character, but give equal time to his attributes. Honestly, objectively examine your part in the situations.

Were you completely blameless? What was your attitude? What were your reactions? What were your choices?

In her Personal Inventory (page 13), Sally wrote that she was angry at her mother for reneging on money she had promised for Sally's new house. When asked to honestly, objectively examine the incident, this is what Sally recalled.

Sally's mother promised to give her money to buy a new house. After putting a binder on one, Sally excitedly telephoned her mother to tell her the good news. Her mother's response was "Are you positive it's a good investment? I'm not so sure. The neighborhood is run-down, the schools are far away, and it's too close to a cemetery."

Sally reacted by yelling at her mother. "So you're not giving me the money. You always change your mind if I don't do things your way." Feeling like a victim, she hung up the phone, cancelled the new house, and hated her mother for disappointing her again.

Upon review of what actually transpired between them, Sally realized that her mother had not actually refused to give her the money for the house. She had only verbalized her fears about the purchase.

This knowledge encouraged Sally to look at the house issue differently. On page 35 please note the negatives and positives Sally listed about her mother as well as Sally's part in the situation and her various choices of responses.

SITUATION *Mother reneged on money she promised.*

MOTHER NEGATIVE: *uses money to control*
always disappoints me
must get her way
doesn't trust my judgment
gives gifts with strings attached
POSITIVE: *worries about me*
didn't actually say no money for the house
wanted to discuss the matter, but I refused

MY PART *I may have misinterpreted her worry as condemnation.*
I told myself there would be no money for the house without giving mother a chance to explain.

MY CHOICES *Get angry, hang up, and cancel house.*
Thank mother for her concern, reassure her that the house is a good investment, and don't mention the money.
Take mother's comments into consideration and look for another house.
Ask mother, "Does this mean you're not giving me the money because you think the house is a poor investment?"
Share with mother, "I'm very disappointed that you don't trust my judgment, and I'm angry because I think you're giving me a gift with strings attached. Please reconsider."

35

As a result of the preceding process, a good portion of Sally's rage toward her mother disappeared because she realized that she was not a victim. She had chosen to be angry and to cancel the house. Next time things could be different.

If you use page 35 as a guide for devictimizing yourself, as Sally and I did, you will begin to accept responsibility for your feelings and see that you have choices.

How do you choose the joy and the peace? To what length will you go to get these wonderful feelings and keep them each day?

I was willing to change my entire belief system.

FLIGHT PLAN SUMMARY OF CHAPTER 1

PHASE ONE   Take a written inventory of our feelings to see what is covering up the real loving us.

PHASE TWO   Acknowledge that we choose these feelings and recognize that we no longer want to hold on to the pain of fear, anger, and guilt.

I CAN FLY
IF I SEE THINGS
DIFFERENTLY

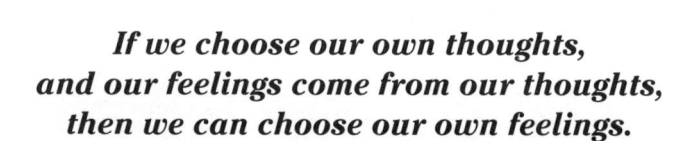

*If we choose our own thoughts,
and our feelings come from our thoughts,
then we can choose our own feelings.*

CHAPTER II

Taking responsibility for everything that I experienced meant changing my entire belief system. I thought feelings were emotions that happened to me as a result of outside influences. I thought I had no choice in the matter. After all, "He made me mad;" "She made me feel guilty;" "What you did hurt me;" and "It's so unfair."

Just as you may, I thought I was the victim. This kind of thinking hadn't worked for me, so with peace of mind as my goal, I became willing to progress to Phase Three in our journey to freedom. I decided to open my mind to some new beliefs. I chose to change my thinking in order to change my life.

Most of us resist giving up our old destructive attitudes as illustrated in this next story:

Larry went to his doctor for a checkup and said, "Doc, I'm dead!"

The physician could not convince Larry otherwise, so he tried a different technique. He told Larry to look in the mirror each day and tell himself, "Dead men don't bleed."

After thirty days, Larry returned to the doctor and told him, "I did what you said, Doc, but I'm still dead!"

With a twinkle in his eye, the physician pricked Larry's finger with a needle and squeezed the blood out.

"Now, what do you think?" he asked.

Larry replied, "Son of a gun, dead men do bleed!"

Don't be like Larry. Leave your resistance behind and come along. All you have to lose is your unhappiness.

YOU DON'T HAVE TO REMAIN A VICTIM

JUST CHOOSE FREEDOM!

CHANGING OUR THINKING IS THE KEY TO OUR FREEDOM

*If we choose our own thoughts,
and our feelings come from our thoughts,
then we can choose our own feelings.*

*In changing our thoughts,
we can now change our feelings.*

Our old thought patterns create everything that we experience. As we go through our lives, we collect experiences to support the things we believe to be true. If we think people disappoint us, we remember bad experiences with people and forget the good ones because this supports our belief that people disappoint us. If we think that we are not good enough, we remember all of our mistakes and forget our successes in order to support our belief that we are not good enough. Whatever we think, we make happen.

I used to wish positively, but think negatively, and wonder why I was so dissatisfied. It was because our thoughts create our reality. If we hold on to negative thoughts, we can actually create weakness in our bodies. Try this exercise:

Have someone stand facing you with one of her arms extended. Ask her to think happy, loving thoughts and to hold out that arm as rigidly as possible. As you tell her to resist, try to press her rigid arm down to her side with one of your hands. It will not budge.

Now ask her to think of someone she hates or of a fearful situation and try again to press down her rigid arm while telling her to resist. This time the arm will fall to her side with only a slight amount of pressure from you.

Now you be the subject and see how the experiment works for you.

You just experienced how bad feelings that come from your negative thinking can sap your energy. Let's examine some of these old beliefs that are the source of all this negativity. (Add your own to the list.)

SOME NEGATIVE BELIEFS

1. People usually abandon and/or reject me.
2. I'm not a nice person, so I don't deserve to look good or feel good.
3. I'm not married, so I can't enjoy life.
4. My parents don't love me, so I'm not lovable.
5. I can't cope with my life without excessive food, drugs, alcohol, or sex.
6. I will never be good enough, rich enough, smart enough, thin enough, or successful enough.
7. I'm unlucky and never get what I want.
8. I'm not a good speaker, writer, or dancer.

Now, let's list behavior patterns that reflect these beliefs. (Add your own to the list.)

ACTIONS THAT REFLECT A NEGATIVE BELIEF

1. If you believe you are not lovable, you may have anonymous sex, no sex, or pick critical, unloving relationships.
2. If you believe that you can't function without compulsive behavior, when you give up one substance, you will substitute another to help you cope with your life.
3. If you believe you will never measure up, whatever you achieve or amass will not be satisfying.
4. If you consider yourself a poor speaker who calls attention to the way he is talking instead of what he is saying, you may speak in a low voice, have poor eye contact, avoid public speaking situations, and often appear inarticulate because of your judgment of how poorly you are speaking. Even when you learn to talk louder, improve your eye contact, or speak publicly, if you still perceive yourself as a poor communicator, you usually will be and others will sense it.
5. If you believe you will be rejected or abandoned, you will rarely share your true feelings or take risks and will probably attract people in your life who are critical and undependable. If you do have loyal and accepting people in your life, you will often misinterpret their actions and feel judged and left out.

When we change only the unwanted behavior without changing our negative beliefs, one of two things will occur. We will soon create new actions to justify these fearful thoughts, or the old behavior will return in order to support the attitude from which it springs. That's why:

After giving up smoking, we compulsively overeat.

After losing weight, we eventually gain it back.
After divorcing an alcoholic, we marry a gambler or another compulsive person.

After moving up the ladder of success, collecting money, trophies, and relationships, we find it's never enough.

Do you want to change your life?

The key is to change your attitudes. Since most of what we think is learned, and anything that is learned can be unlearned and relearned at any time, we can make a decision to unlearn all hurtful thoughts and see things differently. We can think of ourselves in a positive light, as successful, growing people. We can be in charge of our lives.

Let's change our old negative beliefs into positive ones . . . . You can do it!

First, get into a comfortable position, close your eyes and begin to breathe deeply and rhythmically. Focus your attention on the various parts of your body, commanding each part to relax. When you are ready, say aloud as you exhale:

>*I'm willing to let go.*
>
>*I'm willing to let go of my past.*
>
>*I am me.*
>
>*It is safe to be me.*
>
>*I release my limitations.*
>
>*I am willing to open my mind to new beliefs.*
>
>*There is no right or wrong, good or bad; there is only the experience of the moment.*
>
>*I am willing to let go of my old beliefs and be at peace.*

Now we are ready to open our minds and get rid of the old belief that "I don't deserve to look good or feel good." (Or whatever belief you would like to change.)

GETTING RID OF A NEGATIVE BELIEF

Think the negative belief.

Feel it.

Locate the part of your body where you feel it.

Go through the motions of scooping it out and smashing it against an imaginary brick wall.

See it breaking up into little pieces.

In your mind, vacuum up every last bit of that belief, watching it disappear.

Now, imagine a white healing light filling up the emptiness in your body where your belief was.

As you feel yourself bathed in its warmth, say aloud:

> *I rid myself of that old belief forever and I affirm the truth that I am entitled to look good and feel good. (Or whatever you would like to happen.)*

Don't just say it, see it. Experience it in your mind and repeat it each day.

Watch your fears disappear and your self-image improve. As your new thoughts yield positive feelings that will eventually manifest new behaviors, you will become all that you can be.

PERCEPTION IS 100% PROJECTION

PERCEPTION IS 100% PROJECTION

TAKING RESPONSIBILITY

With this new belief system, we have the opportunity to select love over fear and peace over chaos. We can choose life instead of being a victim who blames others for our despair. How wonderful! Instead of wasting our energy trying to control and change other people, we now focus on ourselves because we have finally taken responsibility.

Responsibility means we have decided that our perception of others is 100 percent our projection. For example: When Kathy sees a lack in her friend, Mary, it is really her own lack projected onto Mary. When Kathy sees the beauty in Mary, it is her own beauty that she sees.

If Kathy chooses to see only Mary's strength and love, it reinforces her own. Joy, peace of mind, and happiness are Kathy's because she chooses to see Mary the same way she sees herself. She sees only the good and positive in both—a flowing circle of love, of wholeness and oneness.

If I judge my friend's action as jealousy, it is my jealousy that I see in her. If she doesn't call me often enough and I judge her as lacking consideration for me, it is my low self-esteem that I see.

Her lacking reminds me of mine, and I get angry. If I see her as a caring, beautiful person, it is my feeling beautiful and cared for that I see.

Since I am responsible for my feelings, both good and bad, I try to look at people and accept them totally, without judging. I am able to achieve this because I choose to believe it. When I begin to condemn and criticize, I'm willing to remind myself that my feelings are coming from within myself, not from others.

I know if you're like me, there is probably still a part of you that is fighting this theory. You don't have to agree with me. Just keep an open mind and allow me to explain more clearly what I mean by seeing things differently, selecting love and peace over fear and chaos.

LOVING SPIRIT HUGH SAYS

DON'T JUST READ IT
LIVE IT!

WHAT HAVE I LEARNED SO FAR?

SEEING ONLY LOVE

I choose to believe that we can put our emotions into two categories: love, our natural inheritance, and fear (false evidence appearing real), which is a learned process.

Love is unconditional acceptance and total giving. It recognizes the inner light in each of us. The term love encompasses the positive feelings of bliss, joy, serenity, and freedom. It is the absence of fear.

Fear includes all the forms of our discomfort and negativity; for example: guilt, resentment, jealousy, anger, etc. It is the absence of love. It is the lie that our willful child's voice tells us and that we can choose to believe.

A Course in Miracles teaches that each instant we choose between fear and love; the choice determines the kind of day we have and the way we see the world. For example: If we harbor resentment toward anyone or about anything, we will see the world around us as being fearful and negative. If we extend love, we will see only happiness and good things. The events are the same, but our attitudes about them are different. Again, we create our reality according to our thoughts.

I choose to believe that there is a place within you, within me, within each of us, that is always peaceful, with all kinds of love to express. When you feel joyful, you are experiencing that loving spirit within you. If you meet someone and honestly feel that you are happy to see him or her, you have recognized the love in that person. When someone smiles at you and you smile back, you have reflected the loving oneness in us all.

When we live in the vicious cycle of fear, guilt, and anger, we are not in contact with that spirit of love, which is constant. We are not using this power of unconditional acceptance within us.

When you forget to choose peace and choose anger instead, don't deny the anger. Acknowledge it and say, "Oh, oh! There's that anger again. There's that willful child voice telling me that they are out to get me." Then ask your inner spirit of love for a change of perception. We can get in tune with ourselves and find that quiet place in our minds. We can tap this source of love and see things differently so we are able to look past any unloving attitude of another and see it as a cry for love instead of as an assault. We can change our thinking, which will change our behavior.

In the past, we felt fear and anger when we believed we were verbally attacked. Now, if we change our perception and look at the offensive as a cry for love, we can choose to extend love, if we believe it is possible.

We may hear our children screaming at us. Instead of relinquishing our peaceful state by buying into their anger and defending ourselves or yelling back, which is a typical reaction, we now have another choice. We can ask that loving spirit within us to help us see this experience differently. We don't need to do anything but ask. When the truth is sought in this manner, it is revealed that our children are really loving, as we are, because we are all the same. It isn't worth our getting upset. They may be complaining or criticizing us, but they really want love from us. Our function is to extend that love, for that is who we truly are.

The expression of love will be uniquely appropriate to each of us in accordance with our individual personalities and with each situation. For example: A teenager is using drugs and repeatedly steals money from his family, refusing to go to school or to seek professional help. One parent may be guided to say and do nothing. Another may receive the message to tell the child, in a loving manner, that he must move out of the house. Someone else may calmly call the police and have his son arrested for theft. They all trust that their decisions, coming from a loving, peaceful space, will work out for all parties concerned—and they usually do.

On page 35 Sally had many choices of ways to respond to her mother's unloving attitude. On page 31, many alternatives to Bob, Bella, Jeff, and Sid's dilemmas were presented. How do we find the "right" choice? There are no right or wrong, good or bad decisions. What works for me may not work for you.

Asking for guidance in the manner just described is a simple way of discovering a course of action that is perfect for each individual. Try it. It works.

CHANGE YOUR PERCEPTION SO THAT YOU CAN SEE ONLY LOVE

CHANGE YOUR PERCEPTION SO THAT YOU CAN SEE ONLY LOVE

Most of my life I felt either unloved or unworthy of love, so to feel and express love in my life is a new experience for me, as it probably is for you.

It's difficult to change old habits. I never thought my beliefs would change. I was shocked to find that as I went through the process I am outlining, my negative ideas did begin to shift. I was shocked to find myself being optimistic. Whenever I found myself thinking my old way, I would say, "Stop it," and affirm the positive.

I still worry and get angry, but less often, and I get out of the negative fast. Sometimes, I have to feel a hurt until it's over. I no longer disguise hurt with chemicals or push it down with food; it passes when I'm ready to let it go without judgment.

When I ask myself in the middle of a rage, "Am I willing to be peaceful?" sometimes I answer, "No, not now," and I revert to old behavior. I can laugh about it, however, because I'm still learning, and I'm still human. My teachers are others and problems with others are my opportunities, using lots of patience, to grow.

I promise you, when we simply make a decision that we want peace as our only goal, rather than temporary feelings of being right, and believe peace is possible, we can experience serenity by choosing love and extending it to others. It doesn't even require understanding.

Just do it!

FORGIVENESS

In order to successfully attain peace, we have to remind ourselves each day that love is the only thing that is real. Everything else is a bad dream. The only way to wake up is to forgive.

Forgiveness is selective remembering. It is recalling the love in others and in ourselves and *nothing else*. By doing this, we correct the error of thinking that guilt, anger, and fear are real. We correct the mistaken view that someone can hurt us or that people and the world are unfair.

By doing this, we give up most of the suffering and anxiety that we used to think we needed to deserve to live. We give up being victims and risk being free.

At this point, experience Phase Four of our journey by practicing forgiveness right now. If you are resistant, call on your loving spirit for help.

Let's refer once more to your inventories of fear, guilt, and anger to methodically forgive each person named on those pages. See only the person's strength and love—nothing else. Who cares about what happened years ago? Choose to feel good. Forget the hurt feelings; choose to believe that they never happened—they serve no purpose except to fill you with resentments.

Let them go! Release them now!

Say
> *I forgive my mother for everything.*
> *I forgive my father for everything.*
> *I forgive my spouse for everything.*
> *I forgive my boss for everything.*
> *I forgive myself, etc.*

Close your eyes and visualize every person toward whom you harbor resentment and anger holding hands in a big circle. (I put myself in the circle, too.) See them all with a bright white healing light encircling their bodies. Breathe in and out deeply. Clear your mind of all your negative thoughts, and just feel your love flowing through you toward them. Look into each person's eyes and see only love. We are all one. The past is gone. Choose to wipe the hurtful feelings out of your mind. All you have is this moment. Feel the joy and peace fill your body as you let go of all your anger, all your guilt, and all your fear.

Say:
> *I release fear.*
> *I release anger.*
> *I release guilt.*
> *I forgive everyone, especially myself.*

After the first time I practiced forgiveness in this manner, the knot in my stomach disappeared. I felt relieved of a tremendous burden of garbage that I had carried around for years, and that had only hurt me.

I even went a step further and approached these people in person and made amends whenever possible.

I told them that I was sorry for my part in the situation, and I meant it. Most of them had forgotten those incidents entirely; others remarked that it was about time I apologized; and another said that he didn't forgive me. I still felt OK because I had forgiven myself and no longer had to be right. Being loving felt much better. With each amend I made, I felt lighter and more beautiful, inside and outside.

Forgiveness will work for you, as it did for me. Miracles began to happen to me as I put my new beliefs into action in my daily life.

FLIGHT PLAN SUMMARY OF CHAPTER II

PHASE THREE   Open our minds to the new belief that we can change our thinking and see only love.

PHASE FOUR   Forgive the people in our lives who we believe caused us pain by simply asking the loving voice within us for help.

DON'T HOLD ON
TO YOUR GARBAGE...
GET RID OF IT WITH FORGIVENESS

BLAST OFF TO FREEDOM WITH MIRACLES

As we trust and listen to the loving voice within us, fear, anger, and guilt miraculously disappear.

CHAPTER III

Every time we heal a relationship with love, it is a miracle. Every time we see things differently so our love can flow, it is a miracle.

I was aware for a long time of the miracles that resulted from practicing forgiveness and love before I tested this practice in my daily life. It was easier to talk about the philosophy of changing my perception than to actually live it, especially when living it meant interrupting myself in the middle of emotional turmoil. I was able to forgive the people in my Personal Inventory, but choosing peace while I am filled with anger is a more difficult task.

With patience and an open mind, I listened to joyful, serene people who were previously angry and chaotic share their miracles, so I knew that it was also possible for me.

Each knot in my stomach that accompanied the anger and guilt in which I still indulged reminded me that the discomfort was my choice. As my pain increased, my awareness increased, and I slowly became ready to surrender my self-righteous resistance.

Then one day I did it. I put my new beliefs into action. I entered Phase Five of our journey. As I trusted and listened to the loving voice within me, fear, anger and guilt miraculously disappeared.

CHOOSING LOVE WILL DISSIPATE THE BLOCK OF ANGER

During a long-distance telephone conversation, my teenage daughter came bursting into the house and demanded my immediate attention. I whispered to her that I was on the phone (in case she hadn't noticed) and asked her to please be patient. Totally ignoring my plea, as usual, she continued to enthusiastically describe the events of her day.

I tried to concentrate on my telephone friend, in spite of the distraction of my daughter's chatter, to no avail. Suddenly, my temples began to pound, and I could feel a rage seething deep within me. I thought, *How dare she be so inconsiderate and so rude! She cares only about herself and her immediate gratification! I've told her a million times that when people are on the telephone she should give them common courtesy and not interrupt them! When is she going to learn?* I was so filled with anger that for a moment I wanted to strangle her.

At that instant, it occurred to me that I had another choice if I didn't want to be in such pain. So for the first time while I was in the middle of a rage, I asked the spirit of love within me for a change of perception.

My daughter continued her monologue and my telephone friend continued talking while I closed my eyes and acknowledged that I was uncomfortable (to say the least). Then I thought, *Help me! I don't have to feel these feelings. That willful child part of me tells me to get angry, but I want to believe that I can be peaceful. Show me how! I open my mind so your loving voice can help me to see this situation peacefully.*

After about one minute, a miracle happened. I opened my eyes and saw my grown child as a little girl crying for love. My anger dissipated as I motioned for her to place her head on my lap and I lovingly stroked her hair, which was unusual behavior for me.

My telephone friend continued chatting, with an occasional acknowledgment from me, while I enjoyed a magic moment of closeness and peace with my precious child.

I was amazed! It was so simple! No lectures or judgments were necessary. There was only peace because I was willing to see things differently.

After about three minutes, my daughter quietly went upstairs to watch TV, her face beaming. I completed my conversation and danced up the steps to ask her, "Now what did you want to tell me?" She replied, with a big smile and a hug, "Never mind, Mom, it's not important." We both felt wonderful.

The miracle was that I was at peace. I was free. I didn't have to teach her a lesson. She had taught me—to choose love. It works, if you work it.

CHOOSING LOVE WILL DISSIPATE THE BLOCK OF ANGER

CHOOSING LOVE WILL DISSIPATE THE BLOCK OF ANGER

CHOOSING LOVE WILL ELIMINATE THE BLOCK OF FEAR

Miracles are happening in all areas of my life, not only in my relationships.

Most of my life, I was a perfectionist, which stemmed from my fears of failing. I seldom attempted any task if I believed I couldn't accomplish it faultlessly. I was so busy concentrating on my achievements that I missed the delight of the process of doing.

How sad that while on a trip I was more concerned with sticking to my itinerary without deviating than with enjoying the exploration of a new countryside, relaxing enough to smell the flowers along the way.

How sad that I rarely wrote, except for an occasional letter under duress, because I believed my sixth-grade teacher's comment, "You're a poor writer, Ellie. I suggest you develop your verbal skills." This opinion was verified by my freshman English professor, who, after enjoying my performance in a college comedy, told me, "You may be a poor writer, Ms. Janow, but you are one hell of an actress!"

Is it any wonder that I was afraid to write? I had been programmed, *Writing means putdown.*

So I read a lot and talked a lot and envied writers. I had so much to say, so much to share, but never dared to express myself by using the written word. Someone might laugh or think that I was less than perfect.

Never once was I willing to risk embarrassment or disappointment if someone judged my writing as inferior. I chose to deny a creative energy within me because I was afraid to fail.

Yet, here you are, reading a book, my own thoughts and feelings organized and written by yours truly, not a ghost writer. Here's how the miracle happened.

Lynn, a friend of mine, who knew I was applying a philosophy of love and forgiveness to my daily life, called me one day to judge me and my new outlook on life. She couldn't believe that someone as intelligent and aware as I am would accept such a naive, Pollyanna, unreal view of the world.

I told her that I understood her objections because I, too, had questioned the usefulness of this simple remedy in a difficult reality. It had been hard for me to change my old attitudes. Unconditional love was against everything I had been taught.

I told her that in the past I was told to argue when I was right until I proved the other person wrong. When someone was inconsiderate, I was taught to let him know about it and to teach him for his own good. I learned not to allow anyone to get away with hurting me.

Dealing with reality in this manner had brought me only grief and pain.

I explained to Lynn that I knew the truth now. I woke up from the dream I thought was reality and saw things differently. I practiced unconditional love, and I learned that I'd rather be peaceful than right. I no longer look at reality as being difficult. It is full of opportunities for me to teach love so that I, too, can learn it.

Lynn still insisted that I was a "crazy lady" and suggested sarcastically that I write a book to share my "sugar-coated cure" with the world.

Her teasing pushed my fear-of-writing button, and I heard myself reply angrily with an old tape, "Oh! I can't write at all, especially not a book!" I realized that I really enjoyed sharing *Miracles* philosophy, but I was afraid that I couldn't do it successfully using the written word. My old "stinking thinking" came back in a rush. I thought, *My worth and value depend on my achievements and what someone thinks. If the book is not great, then I am nothing.*

The anxiety these thoughts produced made me very uncomfortable, and I hung up from talking with Lynn feeling angry that I had the audacity even to think I could write a book and feeling guilty that I didn't have the guts to try.

In the midst of this chaos, I opened my mind, let go of my preconceived notions, and allowed a loving voice deep within me to be heard. It shouted, *Stop it, Ellie! You can do anything that you believe you can do. Close your eyes and change your perception of failure. It doesn't exist if you believe it doesn't. No one has to grade your writing. If you want to write your story, then do it. The success will be in the process and in the gratification you will get from expressing yourself. If the act of writing is not pleasurable, you can stop at any time and learn from the experience. It is not the pot at the end of the rainbow that counts, it is the path you take to get there.*

Success isn't measured in getting a book published or other acclamations of your work, though these are nice. The important thing is that you do it without concern for others' opinions. Success is being who you really are and expressing that self the best way you can each day.

I knew this was the truth, so I took the plunge. I am experiencing a fulfillment, an excitement and satisfaction that I've never felt before. I sit down to write for what I think is five minutes, and five hours pass by. I'm exhilarated with the doing—the fear is gone.

I'm writing, sharing, getting feedback, rewriting, reading, thinking, creating, learning, and reorganizing. I'm flying.

I feel good about this book because it's mine, and I'm writing it the best way I know how—with love and joy.

I called Lynn to thank her for giving me the idea of writing a book. She's still in shock.

CHOOSING LOVE WILL ALLEVIATE THE BLOCK OF GUILT

It is usually not what we feel or do that hurts us, it is our own judgment of these feelings and actions.

Oh, to be able just to feel and be in the moment without self-judgments of, *Don't feel that way, it's not nice. Don't do that, you should be doing this.*

We torture ourselves with guilt because we think we have done something wrong.

My neighbor Florence gained fifty pounds after her son died of leukemia. One afternoon, while she was visiting me, Florence shared that she was giving a party for her father's eighty-fifth birthday. Suddenly, she became livid, yelling angrily, "Can you imagine, my father is a decrepit, senile old man and my wonderful son is gone. I hate him for still being alive."

After she quieted down, she apologized for her outburst. Deprecating herself, she said, "Everyone thinks I'm still suffering because of Joel's passing, but what's really unbearable is the guilt I feel over how much I detest this innocent old man. I'm a terrible daughter!"

I hugged her and told her that I thought she was judging herself harshly. I said, "Given the same set of circumstances, I probably would also hate my father. It's OK to feel that way. It will pass if you allow yourself to feel the feelings without condemning yourself."

"You think my feelings are appropriate? You don't think that I'm a bad person?" she replied. "I've tortured myself for so long. When I'm not drunk on food, the pain of my guilt is overwhelming." Relieved that she had let her secret out, she allowed herself to feel her anger and she wept, probably for the first time without self-judgment.

Within the following year, she lost her excess weight and has kept it off. Perhaps my endorsement of her feelings helped her to accept herself by alleviating some of her guilt. I hope so.

Although my neighbor's story is extreme, we are all like Florence. We think we have done something wrong and need to punish ourselves with guilt.

So if we are all wrong, then who is right?

Right or wrong doesn't work anymore. All it does is make us feel bad about ourselves. If our goal is to be happy, we must see things differently.

I remember the first time I was invited to speak at a seminar that involved a weekend away from my husband and children. I wanted to go, but I judged my desire to go as selfish and inconsiderate behavior—it wasn't nice.

I believed I had two alternatives: Stay home and be a good wife and mother, which would make me resentful because I couldn't do what I really wanted to do, or go away and probably feel guilty. I believed that it was OK for me to go away as long as I felt guilty about it because I was being punished for my wrong behavior.

I was a victim; either way my willful child voice said, *Feel bad.*

I chose to go with guilt and had a "suffering good time." That certainly didn't work.

The following year, I was invited to speak again. This time my new philosophy opened my mind to hear a glimmer of a serene voice within me. It allowed me to see other alternatives besides staying home with anger and resentment or going with guilt. I could also choose to go guilt-free or to stay home with love.

I asked the spirit of love within me for guidance and the answer came loud and clear. I realized that I didn't need to use guilt anymore because I wasn't doing anything wrong by going away without my family. I deserved just to go and enjoy: no more judgments, no more punishments, no more right or wrong. The voice reassured me that I was OK and a good person, whatever I chose to do.

I decided to go to the seminar without guilt.

When I revealed my plans to my family, my husband expressed disappointment because I wouldn't be able to accompany him to a business dinner-dance that same weekend, and my children were annoyed that I wouldn't be available to chauffeur them to their various activities. Their objections were vented angrily.

Although my decision caused a lot of chaos in the household, I didn't feel guilty or uncomfortable about my plans. My peaceful feeling reassured me that I was responding to the loving spirit within me and not the willful child voice to which I sometimes mistakenly listen when I want my way.

I can tell the difference because when I listen to my willful child, I have doubts, guilt, anger, and/or fear. I get into trouble. I usually learn and grow from the mistake, so it's not catastrophic. When I listen to my loving spirit, however, I *know* all is well as I carry out my decisions lovingly.

So I told my family that I was sorry they would be inconvenienced, and I was able to go away without guilt and without their endorsement. It felt good. I endorsed myself and became free.

The outcome was happy for everyone. My husband decided that he didn't want to go to the dinner-dance without me and chose to go to Florida for the weekend to visit his parents instead. My children discovered the independence of public transportation and the joy of cooking. I returned relaxed, renewed, and fulfilled.

We can learn from this experience. We no longer have to use guilt to make ourselves feel bad.

We can say no to friends or family members, risk their disapproval, and choose not to feel guilty because we know that we are OK.

When we decide to overeat, stay home from our job or school, be working mothers, or procrastinate, we can take responsibility for these actions and enjoy them. If we indulge in the above behaviors and still feel guilty, at least we can realize the pain is our choice and learn from it. Maybe next time we will tap our inner source of love to see things differently (pages 54 and 55) before we act on anything that is guilt-related.

When we choose love, we either will not indulge in the "misconduct" or elect to do it peacefully. Either way, we will be free of the pointless, self-inflicted torture of our guilt. Try it. It works.

WE CHOOSE GUILT AND FEAR TO MAKE US FEEL BAD

WE CHOOSE GUILT AND FEAR TO MAKE US FEEL BAD

FLIGHT PLAN SUMMARY OF CHAPTER III

PHASE FIVE   As we trust and listen to the loving voice within us, fear, anger, and guilt miraculously disappear.

LOVING SPIRIT HUGH SAYS

DON'T JUST READ IT
LIVE IT!

KEEP FLYING HIGH

*Just for today, share yourself with others.
Trust your loving spirit to guide you to peace.
Be happy, joyous, and free.
It's time to fly!*

CHAPTER IV

Although our natural state is to be loving and peaceful, because of our learned experiences the habitual state for many of us is to be chaotic and angry. As we get caught up in our daily routines, our destructive ways and negative thinking come back, in spite of successful miracles in our lives.

How can we set aside these habits and remember who we really are? How can we program our minds and bodies for success each day?

The solution can be found in Phase Six of our journey: Practice affirmations, visualizations, and sharing to keep us growing and serene and to remind us to be loving each day.

AFFIRMING OUR PEACE AND FREEDOM

Affirmations are positive thoughts that we choose to put into our consciousness in order to produce particular results. They are based on the theory that our minds are computers; if we give them the same information enough times, they eventually believe it.

We can change our negative thoughts into positive statements and say them each day in front of the mirror, in our cars, in the shower, or waiting in lines. We can write them or put them on tape and listen to them every day. It's a form of brainwashing, and it works.

We have already experienced affirmations when we practiced letting go on page 47 and when we practiced forgiveness on page 60.

Some Examples of Affirmations

Try some that apply to you or make up your own!

> *I deserve to give up my fear, guilt, and anger so that I will be joyful and serene.*

> *I am ready to relax now, to accept the energy that is total love within me and share it unconditionally.*

> *I am ready to take responsibility for all of my feelings, both good and bad.*

I deserve to be gentle with myself if my progress as I change is slow. I strive for progress.

I no longer compare myself to others in order to know that I am good enough.

I am ready to see someone's attack as a cry for love.

I am ready to forgive those I blamed for wronging me, including myself.

I deserve to be my ideal weight and have my ideal job.

I am free to make mistakes and grow.

I am free to risk and to give up controlling.

I am ready to live in the present by giving up old tapes of yesterday and my projections into tomorrow.

I am free to be the spontaneous, loving, creative person I was meant to be.

I am lovable and have everything that I need to be happy.

I would rather be happy than right.

I possess a wonderful capacity to change my perceptions, and I am ready, when I am in pain, to see things differently in order to become peaceful.

I am willing to open my mind and ask my inner spirit of love for guidance.

I am ready to look at people with my heart and not my preconceived notions.

I am ready to release anything that is interfering with my ability to be truly me.

I am ready to give up using food, drugs, alcohol, gambling, or any other compulsive behavior to make me feel good.

I am ready to feel good by helping others.

I deserve to make time for myself because I am important.

I am whole and complete right now. My thoughts are creative. All is well.

Affirmations are thanks ahead of time for problems already solved. For example:

Thank you for my healthy family.

Thank you for my successful business and my prosperity.

Thank you for the cooperation and relaxed atmosphere at work.

Thank you for the happy and fulfilling life of my family members and friends.

Thank you for the romantic, passionate, and sharing relationship I have in my life.

Thank you for the courage and patience I need to overcome my difficulties.

Thank you for my new positive self-image.

Thank you for the willingness to change my attitudes by changing my thinking.

Thank you for the willingness to stay sober/sugar-free/drug-free.

Thank you for the peace throughout the world.

Thank you for all my nurturing and loving friends.

Thank you for the ease with which I express my feelings.

Now try some of your own affirmations.

VISUALIZING OUR SERENITY AND JOY

Visualizations are adjuncts to affirmations.

Close your eyes and "see" mental pictures of yourself in your ideal situations. If you are not able to visualize, cut out pictures of yourself when you were happy. Cut out magazine pictures of models in situations you want for yourself. Paste your photo over the models' faces. Look at the pictures each day.

Whatever we want for other people or for ourselves, we can visualize.

> We can visualize our ailing parent smiling, serene, and accepting. The essence of the person is not her deteriorating physical body, but her loving spirit, which is whole and complete.
>
> We can visualize our troubled friends and relatives as problem-free, happy, and peaceful.
>
> We can visualize the world at peace and all people healthy and joyful.
>
> We can visualize ourselves as patient, loving human beings, concentrating on the positive side of life.
>
> We can visualize ourselves saying, *Who asked me?* when we interfere in other people's business.

We can visualize ourselves laughing and saying, *So what, it doesn't matter,* when there's a flood in our basement or a business deal falls through.

We can visualize ourselves saying, *Wait a minute, what is going on here? I don't understand!* in order to give ourselves time to collect our thoughts and ask for guidance instead of reacting to a verbal attack.

We can visualize ourselves saying, *Why not?* when we are afraid to try something new and different.

We can visualize ourselves saying, *It's important that I learn something here,* when we have made mistakes or feel pain or things are not going our way.

A more powerful visualization is a hologram (a three-dimensional picture) centered in the middle of our brain that embodies the five senses of smell, sight, sound, taste, and touch. For example: An athlete who wants to win not only sees himself winning, he can hear the crowd cheering and feel the tape on his chest as he crosses the finish line. He can taste and smell the champagne at his victory party.

A visualization is so powerful because our minds cannot tell the difference between the actual experience and one that is vividly imagined.

Whenever we feel tense, we can visualize ourselves on a tranquil beach or sailing on a catamaran, hair blowing in the gentle breeze, or whatever scene will relax us.

We already experienced this kind of visualization when we rid ourselves of our negative beliefs on page 48 and envisioned the forgiveness circle on page 61.

Every morning I do aerobic disco-dancing for thirty minutes. I started two years ago with five minutes and have gradually extended the time. After I enjoy the music and the feel of my body moving to the rhythm (usually during the first ten minutes), I picture myself as a healthy person, satisfied with the three nourishing meals I plan to eat that day. I also imagine myself driving in my car to unfamiliar places, full of self-confidence and trusting that I will get to my destination safely. I put a family member or friend in the passenger seat, and as we tell each other, *I love and accept you just the way you are,* I see and experience the rays of the sun shining through the windshield, bathing both of us in warmth.

Another fun exercise that I do to cheer me up while I'm dancing, especially when I wake up grouchy, is to go through the alphabet and for each letter find a positive adjective that begins with the letter to describe myself.

For example, *I am*:

abundant	*marvelous*
beautiful	*nice*
centered	*optimistic*
delicious	*positive*
enthusiastic	*quick*
exciting	*resilient*
fun-loving	*satisfied*
gentle	*thoughtful*
honest	*understanding*
independent	*vivacious*
joyous	*youthful*
kind	*zestful*
lovable	

When you do the above mental imagery, act as if these adjectives truly describe you. Feel your abundance. Feel your enthusiasm, and know that if you believe, this becomes your reality.

I don't know exactly when my beliefs changed. However, I do know that today I am driving long distances without my old fear of getting lost. I have miraculously maintained a trim, athletic body, and the need-satisfying dependencies in my life have changed into quality, caring relationships based on unconditional love.

These systematic reminders, affirmations and visualizations, are tools to help us remember who we are and what our function is. We are loving people and our purpose is to extend that love. The best way to extend is through sharing.

WHATEVER
WE WANT FOR OURSELVES
WE CAN VISUALIZE AND AFFIRM

SHARING OUR GROWTH AND LOVE

Most of us are afraid to share because we believe that if "they" knew how imperfect we are, "they" would judge us as being unworthy and "they" would leave us.

We compare ourselves to others: we are smarter, prettier/handsomer, more athletic, better wives/husbands; we are worse mothers/fathers; we have less attractive bodies or have poorer senses of humor. We don't listen to what anyone says to us because we are too busy thinking of our responses and the effects they have.

We spend a lot of time judging, and we rarely trust anyone with our secrets because we are sure that we will be judged in return. We don't want to let anyone know who we are inside because then it could be used against us. We are on guard constantly, ready to defend ourselves or to impress anyone in order to preserve our fragile self-images. Protecting ourselves can become exhausting.

The first time I experienced sharing, the meeting of the minds communicating heart to heart in the moment, was overwhelming.

It was at a small meeting for overeaters. A woman I will call Gloria stood up and shared with the group how difficult it was to cope with her teenage children. She told us about her son, who was dropping out of high school, and how she believed that her dreams and plans for him were being shattered. She shared, in tears, that she couldn't stop eating out of frustration because she couldn't make him realize that he was ruining his life.

I was surprised that she trusted strangers with such a personal story, which I thought should not be public knowledge.

Another speaker, who followed Gloria, started out with the words, "I understand." Without giving advice or making judgments, she told us how four years ago, her son had dropped out of school. She, also, had eaten out of frustration. She found out, however, that eating didn't solve her problems but only added one more heartache to her life. She shared how her son had struggled with his identity, how he had gotten a high school equivalency certificate and is now in college. He is not pursuing the career she had intended for him, but something that he wants for himself. She shared with hope and optimism that she is now sugar-free, and is working on herself instead of depending on her son to fulfill her dreams.

Her honesty brought tears to my eyes as I related to the feelings of both women. The plans, hopes, and dreams we have for our children, and the way we must let them go to become who they want to be, were our common bonds. I went over to Gloria and the other speaker and thanked them for their sharing. It had helped me. Because they shared their uniqueness so openly with me, I trusted them with mine. I opened up and risked telling them my story. The relief was remarkable!

The flow of love, through the bond of shared feelings and understanding was unmistakable. I had thought that I was the only one suffering the pain of letting my teenage children go. Only through sharing, feeling safe with others, letting down my masks and allowing myself to listen to their experiences, could I grow and learn and become myself.

Since that time, I have involved myself with people through a sincere interchange of thoughts and feelings. This requires taking a risk, and sometimes I get hurt when someone judges me. Occasionally, without realizing it, I may hurt another by judging him. We are all in the process of growing. I use these times as opportunities to learn, and I always bounce back.

When we risk sharing, we are truly alive. I have forced myself to risk saying hello to people I have never met, to put my hand out and risk involvement. I have risked being there unconditionally for friends, family, and strangers in need. I have discovered miraculously that in helping them, I was really helping myself. Whatever I want from anyone, I have risked offering first. For example: I have made the first phone call, or said "I'm sorry" and "I love you" first.

I have risked expressing my real self to people I thought loved me only as long as I didn't disappoint them. I became vulnerable and told my feelings to these people, and they listened and accepted me anyway.

I not only have shared smiles and kind words with waiters/waitresses and salespeople but have been able to give up my place in line at the supermarket to someone in a hurry instead of racing with my shopping cart to be first at the cashier, knocking over anyone in my way. That's a miracle!

Sharing affirms the spiritual connection in us all. When we share, we are together right now. We are not worrying about what we are missing or if the other person approves of us. We are listening to each other with our hearts.

When we interact, we allow each other our points of view through a dialogue in which both parties win.

The words we speak have energy and are powerful because we accept as true that which we hear repeatedly. So be aware of the expressions that you use often. Language can work for us or against us. Phrases such as "I can't," "you are wrong," "I should," "if only," "yes—but," "you made me" keep us in the past and reinforce our negative beliefs.

As you share, use positive, noncritical words such as "I can," "I will," "I feel," "I understand," and "I'm sorry you feel that way." Remember that what you give to another is a gift to yourself, so be generous with your praise. If you think someone is worthy of appreciation, tell him or her.

As we exemplify kindness and support in our sharing, we will attract nurturing, loving people into our lives. Our critical, negative relationships either will change eventually or those people will leave us to find others who will play their unloving victim games.

We can keep flying high by discovering who we are and sharing it with others. When we get feedback, it either reinforces our path or helps us question our beliefs, which may lead to changes.

If you feel confused or lonely or unsure of yourself, and you can tell someone about it without shame, knowing the other person is just like you, that is the epitome of sharing.

There is no emotion you have experienced that I have not felt. If we trust in the spirit within each of us and reach out, we will help each other remember that our feelings are not facts. It will make us free.

I was an emotional cripple. People shared their experience, strength, and hope with me and loved me back to health. I discovered that I am a worthy person with something to offer, just as you are. With our new way of thinking, all things are possible to accomplish. Through sharing, we can look at the barriers that block our loving spirit. We can find the power of love within us by tearing away the myths that we believe in: fear, anger, and guilt. They will still come back; when they do, we share them and remind each other that we can choose love instead.

As we extend that love, it feels wonderful. People who feel good about themselves for the first time don't destroy themselves with food, drugs, gambling, alcohol, or anger anymore. They use their energy instead to travel in the circle of freedom. That's a miracle!

We can keep feeling good by practicing Phase Seven, which is filling out the Daily Positive Checklist (page 104) to record and appreciate our process of growth.

Just for today, share yourself with others. Trust your loving spirit to guide you to peace. Be happy, joyous, and free. It's time to fly!

FLIGHT PLAN SUMMARY OF CHAPTER IV

PHASE SIX Practice affirmations, visualizations, and sharing to keep us growing and serene and to remind us to be loving each day.

PHASE SEVEN Make a Daily Positive Checklist to record and appreciate our process of growth.

LOVING SPIRIT HUGH SAYS

DON'T JUST READ IT
LIVE IT!

DAILY POSITIVE CHECKLIST

STATEMENT: *Today I feel good about…*

MY KINDNESS TOWARD

MY FORGIVENESS OF

MY SERENITY WHEN

MY LOVING ATTITUDE TOWARD

MY ACCEPTANCE OF

MY POSITIVE OUTLOOK ABOUT

MY OPEN-MINDEDNESS IN REGARD TO

MY WILLINGNESS TO IMPROVE MYSELF WHEN

MY PHYSICAL ATTRIBUTES OF

MY ATHLETIC ABILITIES IN _____
_____

MY RELATIONSHIPS WITH _____
_____

MY SENSE OF HUMOR WHEN _____
_____

MY IMAGINATION WHEN _____
_____

MY HONESTY ABOUT _____
_____

MY GENEROSITY WITH _____
_____

MY PATIENCE WITH _____
_____

BEING HELPFUL TOWARD _____
_____

MY LEISURE-TIME ACTIVITY WHEN _____
_____

DAILY POSITIVE CHECKLIST

STATEMENT: *Today I feel good about...*

MY JOB/PROFESSION BECAUSE
_____
_____

MY TOLERANCE OF
_____
_____

MY KNOWLEDGE ABOUT
_____
_____

MY WILLINGNESS TO TAKE A RISK WHEN
_____
_____

MY WILLINGNESS TO ASK FOR HELP WHEN
_____
_____

SHARING MY FEELINGS ABOUT
_____
_____
_____
_____
_____
_____
_____
_____
_____

EPILOGUE

THE CHANGELING EAGLE

In a Native American legend, a brave found an eagle's egg and put it into the nest of a prairie chicken. The eaglet hatched and grew up with the brood of chicks.

All his life, the changeling eagle, thinking he was a prairie chicken, did what the prairie chickens did.

He scratched in the dirt for seeds and insects to eat. He clucked and cackled. And he flew with a brief thrashing of wings and flurry of feathers no more than a few feet off the ground. After all, that's how prairie chickens were supposed to fly.

Years passed and the changeling eagle grew very old. One day, he saw a magnificent bird far above him in the cloudless sky. Hanging with graceful majesty on the powerful wind currents, the bird soared with scarcely a beat of its strong golden wings.

"What a beautiful bird!" said the changeling eagle to its neighbor. "What is it?"

"That's an eagle, the chief of the birds," the neighbor clucked. "But don't give it a second thought. You could never be like him."

So the changeling eagle never gave it another thought and died thinking he was a prairie chicken.

It's all too easy to go through life thinking we're prairie chickens when we're really eagles. But doing so shortchanges us and everyone else. Be what you are. Be all that you can be. Don't stay on the ground when you have it in you to soar.

Anonymous

We are all eagles!

How to Feel Good About Ourselves and Our Relationships in Seven Phases

ONE Take a written inventory of our feelings to see what is blocking the real loving us.

TWO Acknowledge that we choose these feelings and recognize that we no longer want to hold on to the pain of fear, anger, and guilt.

THREE Open our minds to the new belief that we can change our thinking and see only love.

FOUR Forgive the people in our lives who we believe caused us pain by simply asking the loving voice within us for help.

FIVE As we trust and listen to the loving voice within us, fear, anger, and guilt miraculously disappear.

SIX Practice affirmations, visualizations, and sharing to keep us growing and serene and to remind us to be loving each day.

SEVEN Make a Daily Positive Checklist to record and appreciate our process of growth.

The terms "he" and "she" were used arbitrarily and intermittently throughout this text to present this work in a nonsexist manner.

Many thanks to those who have read this book and live its message.

If you would like to help spread the beautiful philosophy of love expressed in A Time to Fly, *we suggest that you tell your friends about it.*

It's a Wonderful Gift of Love!

For information about Ellie's workshops or tapes, contact:

ELLIE JANOW
8510 BAY PARKWAY
BROOKLYN, NEW YORK 11214
(718) 996-4600

OTHER BOOKS FROM CELESTIAL ARTS

LOVING RELATIONSHIPS by Sondra Ray
How to find, achieve, and maintain a deeper, more fulfilling relationship with your mate. $7.95 paper, 178 pages.

LOVING RELATIONSHIPS II by Sondra Ray
In this entirely new companion volume, Sondra shares her discoveries as she continues to investigate the secrets of life, love, and spirituality. $9.95 paper, 192 pages.

I KNOW FROM MY HEART by Jack Schwartz
A collection of essays, meditations, and teachings that draw on both Eastern and Western spiritual traditions. *What most delights and amazes me in the life, the wisdom, and the teachings of my friend (Jack Schwartz) is the way in which his words so often illuminate for me the sayings of the greatest masters.*—Joseph Campbell. $12.95 paper, 160 pages.

IT'S NOT WHAT YOU EAT BUT WHAT EATS YOU by Jack Schwartz
After seeing what Jack Schwartz can do to/with his body, you've got to be interested in what's going on in his mind.—Richard Bolles, author of *What Color is Your Parachute.*
An exploration of the intense mind/body connection between nutrition and vitality. $8.95 paper, 224 pages.

THE MAGICAL CHILD WITHIN YOU by Bruce Davis, Ph.D.
Building upon Gestalt Therapy, Transactional Analysis, and Primal Therapy, Dr. Davis provides a disarmingly simple and delightfully written look at self-awareness and love. This book shows how to find and nurture the magical child who lives within each of us. $7.95 paper, 128 pages.

THE ART OF RITUAL by Sydney Barbara Metrick & Renee Beck
A guide to creating and performing personalized rituals for growth and change. The authors discuss the importance of ritual in traditional cultures, and show how to integrate it into modern life, celebrating births, achievements, special friendships, and the like. $11.95 paper, 152 pages.

CHOOSE TO BE HEALTHY by Susan Smith Jones, Ph.D.
The choices we make in life can greatly increase our health and happiness—this book details how to analyze one's choices about food, exercise, thought, work, and play, and then use this information to create a better, healthier life. $9.95 paper, 252 pages.

CHOOSE TO LIVE PEACEFULLY by Susan Smith Jones, Ph.D.
By nurturing our inner selves and living in personal peace, we can help to bring about global change. In this book, Susan Smith-Jones explores the many components of a peaceful, satisfying life—including exercise, nutrition, solitude, meditation, ritual, and environmental awareness—and shows how they can be linked to world peace. $11.95, 320 pages.

LOVE IS LETTING GO OF FEAR by Gerald Jampolsky, Ph.D.
The deceptively simple lessons in this very popular little book (over 1,000,000 in print) are based on *A Course in Miracles;* working with them will teach you to let go of fear and remember that everyone's true essence is love. Includes daily exercises. $7.95 paper or $9.95 cloth, 144 pages.

HEALING THE ADDICTIVE MIND by Lee Jampolsky, Ph.D.
The first book to use lessons from *A Course in Miracles* as a tool for overcoming addictive behaviors, including chemical dependency and codependent relationships. Includes daily exercises for overcoming harmful patterns and gaining spiritual peace. $9.95 paper, 172 pages.

UNLIMIT YOUR LIFE by James Fadiman, Ph.D.
How to assess and understand the factors holding you back in life, and then set concrete goals and start working towards attaining them in the most effective, life-affirming fashion. $9.95 paper, 224 pages.

SELF ESTEEM by Virginia Satir
A simple and succinct declaration of self worth which serves as inspiration and affirmation for anyone who needs a "quick hit" of positive feelings. $5.95 paper, 64 pages.

Available from your local bookstore, or order direct from the publisher. Please include $2.50 shipping & handling for the first book, and 50 cents for each additional book. California residents include local sales tax. Write for our free complete catalog of over 400 books, posters, and tapes.

> Celestial Arts
> Box 7123
> Berkeley, CA 94707

For VISA or MASTERCARD orders call (800) 841-BOOK